W9-CAI-105

Wild Horses I Have Known

Wild Horses I Have Known

Text and Photographs by

Hope Ryden

Clarion Books • New York

MANHASSET PUBLIC LIBRARY

With gratitude to the citizens of
Lovell, Wyoming,
for the many battles they have fought on behalf of
the Pryor Mountain wild horse herd.

Clarion Books
a Houghton Mifflin Company imprint
215 Park Avenue South, New York, NY 10003

Copyright © 1999 by Hope Ryden

Text is 12-pt. Janson.

Book design by Richard Granald.

All rights reserved.

For information about permission to reproduce selections
from this book, write to Permissions, Houghton Mifflin Company,
215 Park Avenue South, New York, NY 10003.

Printed in Singapore.

Library of Congress Cataloging-in-Publication Data
Ryden, Hope.
Wild horses I have known / Hope Ryden.
p. cm.
Summary: Text and photographs depict mustang behavior as observed by the
author, as well as an account of how the mustang has established itself and
adapted to being a wild horse in the American West.
ISBN 0-395-77520-5
1. Mustang—Juvenile literature. 2. Wild horses—
West (U.S.)—Juvenile literature. [1. Mustang.
2. Wild horses. 3. Horses.]
I. Title.
SF293.M3R93 1999
599.665′515′0978—dc21 97-49021
CIP
AC

TWP 10 9 8 7 6 5 4 3 2 1

Contents

Introduction

Once all horses were wild animals. Once there were hordes of wild horses, called tarpans, running all over Europe, Asia, and North America. We know this from twenty-thousand-year-old pictures of tarpans painted on cave walls in France. And we know this from fossilized bones found in North America and Asia.

What happened to all these wild forebears of today's domestic horses?

Regrettably, the last tarpan died in a Polish zoo in 1870. A close relative of the tarpan (with the all but unpronounceable name of Przewalski's horse) may still run wild in a remote part of Asia. It is so endangered, however, that some captive ones are now being bred in zoos.

So what about the mustangs that now populate the American West? Aren't they wild horses?

It depends on how you look at the question. The mustang certainly looks and acts like a wild horse, but the mustang was not always wild. It was once domesticated. It began returning to a wild state around four hundred years ago.

2

Wild Horses I Have Known

Some people reason that because the mustang was once domesticated, it should not be considered a truly wild animal. They refer to it as a feral horse, meaning a stray. Others disagree. They argue that an animal that acts wild, looks wild, and breeds in the wild is wild.

No matter what a person chooses to call the mustang, no one can deny that it is now entirely capable of surviving on its own. Physically, it has undergone changes that better adapt it to a wild, free-roaming life.

For example, many mustangs today are smaller than the average domestic horse. Small horses require less food than do large horses. A small horse, therefore, is more able to survive hard winters and summer droughts than a large horse. Through natural selection, over time, small mustangs have come to outnumber large ones.

Another difference between a mustang and domestic-bred horses is its hard, hard hoof. It is easy to see how having hard hoofs would be important to a wild horse that runs on rocks and never wears shoes. Chipped hoofs can lead to lameness, lameness will slow down a horse, and slowness may result in capture or death.

Physical changes are only part of the mustang story, however. Long-forgotten behavior patterns have also surfaced. Mustang herds now organize themselves into a number of small bands, each headed by a stallion who gathers as many mares as he is able to defend from other stallions. Each stallion then establishes a home range for his band and marks it with his manure piles. As a result, every band has its own pasture, and grazing pressure is spread across a wide area. There is food enough for all.

Other behaviors also operate to insure the future health of a mustang herd. For example, a mustang stallion will drive his female offspring out of his band when they come into their first heat. This prevents the breeding of close relatives, called inbreeding, which could result in deformed offspring.

All the stories in this book reflect long-forgotten horse behaviors that the mustangs have successfully recovered from some ancient part of their brains. And all the stories in this book are true. They are about wild horses I have watched and gotten to know over many years—wild horses that allowed me to observe them in their glorious state of freedom.

And so I say, yes, the mustang deserves to be called a wild horse. By recovering its past ways, it has become our best guide to that time when all horses were wild. At the same time, by expressing its essential nature, it offers us clues and insights into the character of the domestic horses we keep and love today.

To know a mustang is to know what is most true about all horses.

Young Males

Whenever I think of wild horses, I remember Lonesome. He was a Pryor Mountain mustang who at age two was driven out of his birth band by his father. After making several attempts to rejoin this small group of horses that had been his whole world since birth, he gave up trying and traveled alone.

Lonesome was a beautiful animal. He was a dark bay, and he had the most luxuriant black mane I have ever seen on such a young wild horse. It made him appear to be four or five years old, but he was only two and rather small, although his legs were long.

Wild horses do not mature as rapidly as their domesticated counterparts, whose lives are a good bit easier. Wild horses are not fed bales of hay during the long, cold months, when snow falls deep and heavy in the 8,000-foot-high mountains along the Wyoming-Montana border. There winter winds blow with such force that they roil the white tonnage into impassable drifts. So it was not at all strange that Lonesome developed slowly. For five months of the year the grass he needed in order to grow was buried under snow so deep, he had great difficulty digging down to it.

5

Young Males

His first winter, while he still enjoyed membership in his father's band, had not been so hard. Not much snow fell that year, and during cold spells the old stallion, his six mares, and their three youngsters often stood pressed together in one big, tight knot to conserve their body heat. His mother, as it happened, was already pregnant with her next foal and had no more milk for Lonesome, but that didn't matter. Grass had been good that summer and was still available, although blanketed by snow. Whenever the entire band set to pawing, they got down to it in short order.

His second winter was another story. That he survived the bad weather is cause for wonder. Snow never seemed to stop falling, and it turned the high country into a white blank. From the valley below, the Pryor Mountain range became invisible. People there worried that the wild horse herd might be experiencing another winter die-off.

In early April, on the first day the range looked mountable, I headed up its steep slopes with a friend. Rotten snow still clotted what was meant to be a road, and our four-wheel drive slid this way and that as we tried to gun our way through the stuff.

We were in a state of high excitement. How had the horses fared? How many had made it through the winter? Where was the band that normally occupied this or that plateau?

We raised our binoculars and glassed every ridge in an effort to account for all of our old friends. Ah, there was Diamond Jim up on the ridge with one, two, three mares. But where was his old brown one? Was she off having an early foal? We struggled onward and upward. Then, just as we plowed through a drift that all but spun us around, I spotted Lonesome.

I hadn't named him yet, although I knew at once who he was. Even as a yearling still attached to his birth band, this young stud had stood out. His thick mane and forelock were distinctive. Now I saw that he was by himself. What had happened? Had he wintered alone?

Normally, after young males have been expelled from their fathers' harems, they get together and form what are called stud bands. For several years—until they are old enough and strong enough to challenge mature stallions for their harems—these adolescents stick together. In so doing, they acquire important skills. For example, they frequently engage in play fights, which ready each one for the day he will do battle in earnest. They also drive one another about with their necks outstretched, their heads lowered and weaving—body language they will someday use to keep their mares from straying.

Belonging to a stud band provides even more advantages. Members groom one another. They chew cockleburs from tangled manes and forelocks. When flies are thick and biting, any two horses may stand side by side, facing in opposite directions, and use their tails as switches to brush the pesky insects from each other's faces. Moreover, should the need arise to dig out a water hole or plow through heavy snow, many hoofs make the work a whole lot lighter.

But here, standing before me, was something unusual: A young stud colt had apparently weathered a most bitter winter all by himself. How had he managed? As I jumped out of the four-by-four, already talking, he stood stock-still and studied me.

A great deal depends on how I deport myself when a wild horse first sees me. For a few seconds he will freeze in place as he tries to size me up. It is during this brief interval that I make every effort to convey an attitude of nonchalance. Animals, being nonverbal, pick up clues about other animals (including people) by observing their posture and movements. And so I did not look directly at this stud colt. On the other hand, I didn't hide from him. Instead, I kept up a stream of chatter until the young male relaxed.

I always talk to wild horses. They seem to like it. Even after they have come to tolerate my presence, my chatter allows them to keep constant tabs on my whereabouts. It also reassures them that I am not up to something sneaky. A cougar looking for dinner would never behave as I do.

Granted, this strategy doesn't always work. Still, sometimes, instead of spooking and running away at the sight of me, a bunch will stand and study me for a few moments, then go back to pulling grass. When this happens, I silently rejoice and settle in for a day of horse watching. As my subjects move about, I trail behind them at a discreet distance. Only if I edge too close or make too sudden a move will they take flight.

But now Lonesome's behavior was bizarre. He was more than tolerant of me. He made no attempt to maintain even a narrow safety zone around himself. On the contrary, he actually approached me. And the more I talked, the closer he came. Obviously, he was acting out of intense curiosity, yet for him to take such a risk, something more had to be going on in his head. What was it? Could he be seeking the companionship of another living creature?

"Why, you're lonesome," I cried out as he stretched out his neck to sniff me.

7

Young Males

I didn't move a muscle, and when his soft nose bussed my sleeve, I refrained from touching him. Instead, I backed slowly away. I was not afraid. I just didn't want to make a pet out of a wild horse.

That experience set me to thinking about a question that had long puzzled me: How did man first persuade the horse to become his friend, partner, and servant? Or did this alliance come about by mutual consent?

It happened some four thousand years ago, when wild horses, called tarpans, inhabited much of the northern hemisphere. Over thousands of years people had hunted this animal for food, without giving a thought to training it. Then one day (there has to have been a first day) somebody managed to capture and ride a tarpan. In due course the horse became man's partner in war and his means of transport.

But why would a wild horse go along with such an unnatural arrangement? Its cousin the zebra continues to defy all attempts to domesticate it. Could it be that the tarpan was a willing party to its enslavement? If so, what was in it for the tarpan?

Perhaps it happened this way: A young tarpan, after being expelled from his birth band, failed to find other ousted males to run with. Such an individual, lacking companionship, may have hitched up with human beings out of sheer loneliness. And this event may have been repeated many times.

Of course, we can only guess about events that took place more than four thousand years ago. All we can say for certain is that to this day horses, wild or otherwise, do want company. Even the greatest racehorse of all time, Secretariat, traveled from track to track with his old gray stablemate. Without this friend by his side, Secretariat could not be counted on to perform at his peak.

Yes, horses do want company. If ever I had doubts about this, they were dispelled on that spring day in the Pryor Mountains when Lonesome touched me. In that instant I could have slipped a halter on his handsome head and led him off the mountain.

9

Young Males

The Pryor Mountain wild horses have beautiful heads and conformation that attests to a Spanish mustang ancestry.

A mare on her own (right) *is alert for danger. Mares leave the protection of their harems to give birth.*

A harem strings out and follows its lead mare. The harem stallion brings up the rear so he can fend off pursuers.

A blue roan mustang—one of the many colorful wild horses seen in the Pryor Mountains on the Wyoming-Montana border.

The Black King (above) *with his bevy of bays. This stallion prefers brunettes.*

A boundary conflict (right) *between two neighboring stallions is resolved by ritual pawing.*

My old friend Lonesome at age seven with his first mares.

A lone stallion surveys the scene.

A bachelor band (left). *Males seek the company of other males after being evicted from their parental bands at age three. They stay together for several years.*

Stallions

The Black King was not really black—he just appeared so. Actually he was brown-black. A true black horse is a rarity. Not only is his coat black; so is his hide. By contrast a brown-black horse has a light hide, and come summer, his coat fades to a dark mahogany color. But when I first saw and named The Black King, it was early spring and he was black. Afterward the name stuck. It just seemed to suit him.

During the first year I observed this stallion, he possessed a harem of fourteen mares and seven foals. His was the largest harem ever seen in the Pryor Mountain Wild Horse Range. It was unique for another reason too. All but one of his mares were bays, meaning their bodies were brown and their manes and tails were black. The lone exception was a mare whose body was brown like her harem sisters, but whose mane and tail were not black but brown. I had to wonder how The Black King had managed to gather this bevy of brunettes. Had it been deliberate? It certainly would seem so—especially since the mares in nearby bands were predominantly gray, grulla, roan, buckskin, and palomino.

A stallion assembles his harem by several means. He may defeat another stallion in battle and capture all of his mares. Or he may manage to abduct just one mare from the harem of a stallion who is not paying attention. He may also pick up a wandering filly who has recently been expelled from her sire's band.

Obviously, much happenstance is involved in the gathering of a harem, so it would seem unlikely that a stallion would allow color to be a deciding factor. Still, there they were—fourteen look-alike mares! When lined up, they might have been matching parade horses. And line up they did. The Black King was a taskmaster when he wanted his mares to move. In this he was the same as all harem stallions—only more so.

It is the nature of a stallion to be possessive and domineering. If he weren't, he could not keep his mares together and he would lose them. All around are unattached males looking for opportunities to raid a scattered or unguarded harem. To grasp just what a harem stallion is up against, consider the overall makeup of a wild horse herd. Equal numbers of males and females are born into a normal wild horse population. It follows therefore that if one male takes possession of several females, several males will have none. Understandably, these surplus stallions are on the lookout to remedy this situation, and they give the harem stallions no peace.

This makes for interesting horse watching. It can also be somewhat treacherous to a human observer. I should know, because from time to time I have been challenged by nervous stallions. Mostly these confrontations end quickly. The stallion signals his mares to run away while he stands his ground and faces the oncoming threat. Soon, however, he drops his belligerent stance and hurries to catch up with them.

After all, another stallion may be lurking just over the ridge waiting to capture his mares.

Once while watching horses in a Nevada desert, I found myself in a somewhat different situation. The gray stallion who suddenly materialized out of the blue haze and silence and began circling me had no harem to defend. So why was he challenging me?

To keep the wheeling horse in view, I turned around and around, a dizzying experience. At one point I raised my camera and snapped his picture. I should have known better. The click of the shutter alarmed him and he came to a halt, laid his ears back, and eyed me balefully.

Now I was in big trouble. My mind raced. I was alone. I was miles from cover and I was at the mercy of an aroused stallion who could pummel me to dust in a matter of minutes. Strength drained from my body as I stood weakly, my arms hanging limply by my sides, my cameras dangling uselessly about my neck. All I could hope for was that my utter vulnerability might defuse the horse's combativeness.

But the big gray horse snorted and took a step toward me. By then my heart was pounding so hard, I could hear it in my head. Don't panic, I told myself. Don't scream. Don't run.

I tried to make sense of what was happening. Why was this bachelor stallion so combative? He certainly couldn't be viewing me as another stallion. Did he perceive me as a predator? That would be bad news. Wild horses trample coyotes to death. Then it occurred to me that I might have frustrated his efforts to ambush the little band of wild horses I had been photographing all morning. Had I been getting in his way?

23

Stallions

Whatever it was that was annoying him, the gray horse clearly had his dander up. He pulled in his chin until it nearly touched his chest, causing his neck to arch and his big mane to bristle. Then he began to paw the dust with his front hoofs. I well knew the meaning of his behavior. It was a prefight ritual understood by every stallion. It was an invitation to do battle.

Another stallion would have responded in kind. He would have arched his neck, pawed up some dust, and snorted. Then the two would have closed the space between them until their foreheads butted, whereupon they would eyeball each other for some seconds while tensions escalated. Then, abruptly, one or the other would rear and paw the air—a signal that the fight was on. In an explosion of fury and muscle power they would go at each other.

A stallion fight can be fierce. Contestants do battle in an upright position, standing on their hind legs. This allows them to use their front hoofs and their teeth to inflict wounds. From time to time one or the other will drop to the ground, whirl about, and kick the other's head with his hind feet. But he will soon be upright again, maneuvering for an opening to sink his teeth into his rival's neck.

I knew all about wild horse battles. I had seen many. I had even observed challenges that fizzled before any blows were struck. This can happen when a weaker stallion, after sizing up his rival's superior strength, calls it quits. Somehow during the prefight posturing a truce is negotiated. One or the other concedes defeat in advance of battle, and the loser is allowed to leave.

Now I looked for some such way out of my predicament. Running was not an option. Even a month-old mustang foal can outrun an Olympic sprinter. I have clocked a band of wild horses that included two very young foals at thirty-five miles per hour. There was only one thing for me to try. Although my voice sounded as if it belonged to somebody else, I managed to utter a few soothing words to the animal that was menacing me.

At that he raised his head and regarded me with an air of curiosity. Then he blew air through his nostrils to clear them so that he could better pick up my scent.

Years of cooing to my pet dogs must have prepared me for just this day. I kept up a stream of talk, and the horse seemed to listen. I babbled on and on about nothing in particular in the most honeyed tones I could muster, and the stallion pricked up his ears. I kept on chattering until, without warning, my tormentor sounded a shrill whinny and bolted!

Once I was safe, my relief quickly turned into celebration.

"Was it something I said?" I called after the retreating horse.

Of course, the big horse lacked a sense of humor and didn't even whinny. He had spotted the band that I had been tracking all morning and was after them in hot pursuit. He would have his fight after all.

His target now was a sorrel stallion, who saw him coming and was ready to take him on—but not before sending his mares and foals flying. I edged closer and watched as the sorrel forced them to their utmost speed, running close behind them with wagging head. When they reached the crest of a hill, he turned back and headed straight for trouble.

In seconds the gray horse and the sorrel were face to face, and the two arched their necks, postured, and snorted. This ritual was followed by a bloodcurdling scream from the gray stallion. Then both animals reared and began pummeling each other with their front hoofs.

The dust they raised was thick and obscured much of the action, but the sounds of grunts and screams and hoof meeting hide kept me informed of the battle in progress. Then, as suddenly as it had begun, the skirmish was over; the sorrel stallion was making tracks to rejoin his mares, and the defeated gray stood alone.

At that point I decided to make a swift departure, before the defeated horse decided to return and take out his frustration on me. I may have broken a record for speed walking that day. Without looking back and with Paul Bunyan strides, I headed for my pickup, an hour's hike. There I rewound my film and crossed my fingers that the roll would contain a sharp image of my beautiful adversary.

It didn't matter, though. His beauty and elegant posturing were forever recorded in my brain, and I would never, never, never forget him.

A harem stallion stands his ground, giving his mares lead time to escape.

In a battle with bachelor Buck, The Black King takes it on the chin.

A jet black stallion and his beautiful mares.

After his mares suddenly take flight, a stallion tries to locate the cause of their alarm.

A mare stands guard over her newborn foal. She won't rejoin her harem sisters until her baby is able to keep pace with them.

A stallion (third from right) *herds his mares into line.*

Short backs and small feet are typical of Spanish mustangs found in the Pryor Mountains (opposite). *Long strides and a running walk also affirm their Spanish heritage, linking them to the Paso Fino breed.*

A dust bath relieves painful insect bites.

Stallions with Harems

The Black King, for all his aggressiveness, commanded my respect. He did his job well—kept watch over his mares and never allowed them to scatter. When one strayed, he either moved the others to join her or went after her with snaking neck and herded her back into his ranks.

The stallion's herding posture is a harmless means of keeping his mares and foals together. Togetherness is important to a band's safety. Any member that has become separated from the others, even by a short distance, may be singled out and killed by a wild predator. So when The Black King rounded up his mares, he was acting in their best interest. Whether or not he was aware of this is of no importance. It is a stallion's nature to be domineering, and at times he will push his mares around for no obvious reason.

On several occasions I watched The Black King drive his band of brunettes back and forth across the length of his home range in what appeared to be nothing but an exercise of his authority. There was no threat in sight, nor were they going anyplace. Yet he forced them to run single file at top speed. Aimless though this activity seemed, the workout may have been just what the mares needed after a lazy day standing around cropping grass. In any case, it affirmed the lines of authority.

A stallion's possessive behavior is directed not only toward his mares; he lords it over his foals and yearlings too. Until his offspring reach the age of two or three, they are an integral part of his band and he defends them. This was clearly demonstrated on one occasion when I watched The Black King retrieve a colt (a male foal) who had accidentally run off with the wrong band. It happened during a skirmish between The Black King and a neighboring stallion along the border of their adjoining home ranges. While the two males postured and blew and showed off for each other, their respective harems retreated in opposite directions. In all the commotion, one colt became confused and took off with the wrong band.

I waited to see what would happen. Would the colt's mother cross territorial boundaries to retrieve him? Would the neighboring stallion drive the trespassing youngster out?

I didn't have to wait long, for the dispute between the two stallions was quickly settled by ritual rather than by a show of force. Long ago these neighbors had determined who was the stronger, and they no longer bothered to fight it out. After a few flails with their front hoofs, none of which met their mark, the weaker stallion withdrew, whereupon the victorious Black King pranced back to his waiting harem with neck arched.

No sooner had he rejoined them, however, than his posture changed. Something was amiss! Back he streaked into enemy territory, plowing deep into the midst of his neighbor's mares! Quickly he singled out his wayward offspring and off he dashed, snaking the little fellow along in such a burst of speed that I hardly dared to watch. Surely the colt would fall and be trampled!

But no. Though pushed to his limit, the youngster kept up the pace until he reached safety at his mother's side. He must have inherited his sire's stamina.

For most of the year harem stallions maintain a respectful distance from one another, each occupying his own home range. Not only does this arrangement help them avoid encounters that might lead to dangerous combat, it also apportions the available grass so that there is feed for all.

Some ground, however, must be shared. For example, watering holes and the corridors leading to them are treated as communal property, and visits to these areas are staggered. If one band shows up at a spring before another has finished drinking, the new arrivals wait their turn at a safe distance. Thus both timing and spacing are strategies used by horses to keep the peace and avoid unnecessary combat.

Though this sensible code of behavior is observed by harem stallions, it is often flouted by stud bands. These gangs of adolescent males neither stake out land claims nor respect the property rights of harem-possessing stallions. They are lawless vagabonds, roaming at will, poaching grass here, teasing a stallion into chasing them there, and creating confusion and disorder in general. I suppose that's what makes a stud band such fun to watch. Members are exuberant and full of themselves and seem to enjoy making trouble.

One such band spent a good deal of time near the home range of The Black King, and I named them the Bandidos—a Spanish word for bandits. Two members of this juvenile gang hardly looked old enough to be called yearlings, and I wondered why they weren't still at their mothers' heels. Both were bays—one a sandy shade, the other reddish brown like all of The Black King's offspring.

A third Bandido was about four years old. He was a glossy, black beauty with one white sock on his left hind foot and a crooked blaze that trickled down his face like spilled milk. I called this handsome firebrand Blackie.

The fourth member, Buck, was also about four years old. He was a Roman-nosed buckskin with a number of black rings encircling each leg like bracelets. He also had a wide stripe down his back and another one across his shoulders. Such striping shows up in animals born into mustang herds that have been wild for many, many generations. It is a throwback to a primitive coat pattern. The zebra, the wild ass, and the onager wear stripes of one kind or another.

I rarely saw the Bandidos when the sun was high. They were probably making their presence felt higher up in the Pryor Mountain range. But as the sun's rays would begin to slant across the mountains, the four would appear in the valley of The Black King, prancing and snorting.

At such moments I sprang to my feet so I would be plainly visible. The Bandidos were accustomed to my presence and no longer spooked at the sight of me. In fact they ignored me in much the way they ignored deer or rabbits or any other harmless nonhorse in their midst. Once, however, I confused them by sitting down on the ground to rewind my film. A sudden sound alerted me to look up just in time to see Buck charging toward me with his ears laid back.

With a shriek I leaped to my feet—a move that caused him to stop as abruptly as a show horse refusing a jump. He must have momentarily mistaken me for a coyote lurking in the grass or a cougar crouched to spring. This was a valuable lesson for me—a reminder that I was dealing with wild, not tame, horses.

The two older Bandidos, Buck and Blackie, were almost never quiet. When not engaged in mock battle, they played at herding. Both vied to dominate the all-male band. After every skirmish one or the other would assume the herding posture of a mature wild stallion and drive the others about.

The two younger members rarely engaged in such aggressive play. On the contrary, they allowed themselves to be pushed around by one or the other of the older males and seemed resigned to their lowly status.

One evening, while trailing the Bandidos, I noted with some apprehension that they were nearing the home range of The Black King. As they moved across the valley, engaged as usual in high-spirited play, Buck and Blackie made frequent stops to produce long whinnies that seemed to say, "Here I am, I'm alive!" They then would punctuate this declaration by rearing on their hind legs and pawing the air with their forefeet.

I believe that I saw The Black King coming before the Bandidos did. He charged down the slope like a warhorse, and a one-against-four battle erupted, a virtual swirl of horses kicking, rearing, and moving around me. At one point I found myself in the very center of the battle, taking evasive action this way and that. But wherever I leaped, horses were there—pounding, circling, whirling, screaming, and clouting one another with savage kicks.

When I wasn't ducking, I managed to snap a few pictures. At a later date one of these photographs appeared in *National Geographic* captioned "Double uppercut stuns stallion." I had caught Buck's moment of triumph just as his hind feet connected with The Black King's chin.

What happened next I somehow missed seeing. When I turned to look, one of the yearlings was down and The Black King was plucking hair out of his mane with his teeth. With each yank a few strands came out and dangled like a scalp trophy from the stallion's mouth. Then to my amazement the other three horses, instead of coming to their buddy's rescue, also began tearing at the yearling's mane. For a few minutes, while they all chomped on mane hair, the fight was on hold.

What on earth was going on?

It took me a few minutes to realize that the stud colt was not being injured—his attackers were not drawing blood, nor were they trampling him. Had hair pulling somehow become a symbolic substitute for actual biting?

I regarded this incident as possible evidence that wild horses, like many other wild species, may establish pecking orders in which every individual has a ranking. In such animal societies, bystanders sometimes join in the fray and jump on an "underdog."

Surprisingly, the bay yearling seemed to be suffering no harm except to his mane, which was a sorry sight. What was it about his mane that would cause the other horses to stop fighting and mouth it?

Then round two erupted. It was short, lasting only as long as it took

The Black King to rout the three unvanquished Bandidos. As they disappeared from view, I took a look around. The yearling bay stood alone with his head hanging low, and only raised dust marked the spot where all the action had taken place. I packed up my cameras and prepared to leave.

But the conflict wasn't over. When The Black King returned, victorious as usual, he circled the dispirited yearling and then snaked him off to his waiting harem a quarter mile away. I had never seen a harem stallion capture a male horse before. Then it struck me that this young bay could be one of his offspring. He certainly was the right color! What's more, The Black King seemed as content with his spoils of war as if he had just acquired another female. Did he recognize this animal as one of his own?

I was beginning to make sense of the matter. The yearling was too young to have been evicted from his parental band. Had he somehow become separated from The Black King's harem and ended up in a stud band? It would be only natural for him to seek the company of other horses.

But this strange story didn't end there. Horses in a stud band also form bonds with one another. I was about to see how strong those connections can be. Buck, after a short recovery period, apparently missed the young companion he had grown accustomed to bullying. Unaccompanied by the others, he galloped the length of the valley and managed to swing around behind The Black King's harem before he was spotted.

The chase that followed told me everything there was to know about The Black King. He rocketed after Buck as if jet-propelled. The four-year-old ran the race of his life, with The Black King gaining on him at every stride. Pushing himself to the limit, Buck surged ahead, only to flag again and lose ground. He surely would have been overtaken had not The Black King lost interest in the chase, turned, and galloped back to his harem.

I was exhausted by so much action. The Black King, on the other hand, showed no sign of fatigue. Upon reaching his home range, he circled his now slightly enlarged band and began herding it back and forth from one end of the valley to the other.

It was time for a drill.

43

Stallions with Harems

A lone stallion.

An aggressive display meant to warn away an approaching stallion.

An out-and-out battle erupts between two harem stallions when they encounter each other at a stream. Normally, bands stagger their visits to water to avoid such conflicts.

Although the two stallions are evenly matched, the pinto will ultimately win the day. Meanwhile, their mares look on dispassionately.

A stallion elongates his neck, lowers his head, and wags it from side to side. This action signals his mares to get moving.

An adolescent male practices herding his male companion. This is a skill he will someday need when he possesses a harem of mares.

After a short separation, two bachelor studs touch noses in greeting.

Young studs engage in a mock fight—a sport that readies them to take on harem stallions and win mares.

A high stepper. Wild horses run on rocky terrain and learn to pick up their feet. This natural action calls to mind the exaggerated gait of a trained Tennessee Walking Horse.

Look-alike half-siblings enjoy one another's company in the security of a harem. Born to different mothers, they resemble their common father.

Mares

Old Nellie was a sorry sight. Her back was swayed and her belly sagged. In addition, her coat was scarred and sparse and her mane and tail were scraggly. She called to mind that wretched horse of song: "The old gray mare, she ain't what she used to be." And indeed Nellie was not at all what she used to be when I first came to know her many long years ago. Then she was in her prime and almost beautiful. She was also the lead mare in her band, the queen of the harem.

It comes as a surprise to many horse watchers to learn that the lead mare acts as the brains of a harem. The stallion, for all his brawn and bossiness, does not determine where his string of mares and foals will head when he signals them to get going. It is his job to be aggressive—to stand his ground and hold off all threats while his mares and foals head for safety. Where and how the mares and foals make their escape is decided solely by the band's chief strategist, the lead mare. It is an awesome job. The lives of all the members of the harem depend on her knowledge of the landscape and her good horse sense.

What special qualities must a good lead mare possess?

Besides knowing the lay of the land, she must be cautious and avoid leading the bunch into a dead-end canyon, where all could be trapped. At the same time, she must be bold enough to select escape routes too difficult for pursuers to negotiate. Few animals are as sure-footed as the wild horse. Finally, she must keep in mind the makeup of the band so as not to lead the harem foals to the brink of a chasm that they cannot jump.

I have watched a good lead mare lose a pursuer (me) by galloping down a canyon trail so steep that it would give pause to a mountain goat. Yet the other harem mares, together with their stallion, who was bringing up the rear, did not hesitate to follow her in that headlong flight. Herds that have survived to the present probably have contained many such dauntless females.

How or why one mare, rather than another, becomes a harem leader is not known. It is unlikely that the matter is settled by force, for all-out battles between females have rarely been reported. Nor is it probable that the lead mare has somehow been designated for the job by the other members of the harem. Often she isn't very likable, for she tends to be bossy, nipping any mare who gets in her path, and asserting her right to drink first at watering holes. My best guess is that she casts herself in the lead role. From what I have seen, she could hardly do otherwise. Her responses are so quick, her sense of herself so large, and her knowledge of the landscape so certain that she's off and running before the others know what's up. As a result, they string out in a long line and follow.

You might get the impression from all this that harem life is not very pleasant for mares. It is certainly true that they are frequently badgered, led, driven, and herded. Nevertheless, on most days harem life is serene. The stallion's constant vigilance seems to free all the others from having to be on constant guard, thus allowing them to focus on other matters. Friendships are formed between and among harem members. These bonds can be so strong that one mare may even accompany another when she takes temporary leave of the harem to give birth.

I love to watch members of a wild horse band interact. Mares groom one another, yearlings engage in mock fights, foals frolic. Often during the day new mothers stand as still as rocks, each one positioned alongside a sleeping baby. When a foal wakes up, its mother busies herself nibbling, caressing, and nursing the youngster.

To a horse, touch is an important sense, and body contact is frequently used to communicate mood. Mutual grooming occupies part of every day and serves to reinforce good relations between the groomers. Sometimes several harem members huddle together, thereby shielding the contact points of their bodies from biting insects. Or they may form a wheel, facing inward, and use their tails as fly swatters.

When flies are particularly bothersome, members of a band will roll on the ground. Caked dirt provides good insulation against stinging insects and may even have a soothing effect on bites. Sometimes a band will head for high ground, where strong winds blow away their tormentors. Of course, the lead mare knows and shows the way to these pest-free pinnacles.

Obviously harem life provides security, structure, and social contact for mares and their young, and I suspect all this is to their liking. Just as ousted stud colts seek one another's company and form gangs, so mares seem to find comfort in being with other mares. Their tendency to socialize may, in fact, be the glue that holds each band together. Though it is the stallion who assembles and dominates a harem, he would have great difficulty holding on to mares who were antagonistic toward one another and inclined to disperse.

It is odd that the stallion, who is normally so possessive of his mares, seems not to notice when a pregnant female slips away to give birth. Does he sense that she will return on her own? Maternity leave lasts only as many days or weeks as it takes a newborn to gain strength enough to keep up with his mother's band. Then she leads the baby back to her harem.

On that day there is much excitement. Mares and yearlings crowd about and nose the little stranger. Even the stallion shows keen interest in the new addition to his band. Most of his attention, however, is focused on the mare. Likely he has sensed her absence, for he usually greets her return with loud nickers.

While foals are very young, they stick close beside their mothers. Fillies (female foals) are more inclined to behave in this way than colts (male foals) are. Before long, however, all the harem youngsters, male and female alike, become interested in one another and engage in wild bouts of play—racing, sparring, kicking up their heels, and nibbling each other's brushlike manes. Such horsing around occurs in short spurts throughout the day. In between times the foals return to their mothers for nourishment and to rest, for they tire easily.

Most mares are excellent mothers, mindful of their babies. In a few cases, however, an inexperienced mare may be inattentive. One such laid-back mother, a beautiful dove-colored grulla, failed to notice when her male offspring suddenly decided to check me out at close range. Throughout the morning I had been photographing the band from a nearby slope, while its members had kept a wary eye on my whereabouts. Then, just as the adults seemed to relax their guard a bit, the curious colt headed straight toward me.

My first thought was to back away as fast as I could. I certainly didn't want to find myself between a mare and her foal! But to my surprise the grulla mother simply glanced up, noted where her youngster was headed, then went back to cropping grass. Well, I thought, since she doesn't seem to mind, I'll just use this opportunity to shoot a few close-up pictures of him.

And so I fired away at the leggy youngster as he stalked closer and closer. I know now that in such a circumstance I should not have kept one eye closed and the other one pressed to my viewfinder. Out of nowhere loomed a black mare, her ears laid back and her teeth showing. With no cover in sight I had little choice but to hold my ground, which I did with pounding heart. But I was not her target. With a nip the mare brought the errant colt to a surprised halt just as he stretched out his neck to sniff me. And she continued to nip and bump him along as she drove him all the way back to his negligent mother.

And who was this rescuer from nowhere? Why, none other than

Old Nellie! Although she was no longer producing foals of her own, the decrepit erstwhile lead mare had taken it upon herself to round up another mare's foal.

Wild mares have a rather long foaling season. Birthing begins in April, peaks in May, and tapers off in June. After that it is a rare and out-of-sync mare who drops a foal. Late-born babies do not stand much chance of growing big enough and strong enough to make it through the oncoming winter. On the other hand foals born too early in the spring may arrive during a late snowstorm. By staggering births over a ten-week period, nature has insured that at least some foals will survive.

Despite this relatively long foaling season, I rarely have stumbled onto a mare during or just after she has given birth. Mothers-to-be choose carefully where they will drop their babies so they will not be discovered by a predator.

Once, however, I spotted a mare with a newborn foal directly across a deep chasm. I was at the same level as the two of them and only a short distance away as the crow flies. On foot, however, it would have taken me a half hour to reach them, and the mare seemed to know that. She didn't bother to nudge her tottering infant to another hiding place, so I sat down and spent the rest of the day watching them.

Newborn foals have no small problem finding the right place to suckle. Their shaky legs frequently give out under them, sending them, splat, to the ground. Eventually, though, they hit upon a nipple and take in their very first nourishment. Then, exhausted by the effort, they sink to the ground and go to sleep.

The foal of the mare I was watching charmed me by doing exactly that. But it was the mare herself who held my interest. How patiently she stood guard over her baby. From time to time she gently nuzzled him. And whenever he struggled to be upright, she turned sidewise and cocked her hind leg slightly to help him find the place he sought. It was a peaceful scene, and I was so touched by her tenderness that I decided to name her Angel.

For several hours I sat quietly, feeling in tune with the world. Yet I was bothered by a question: What kind of future would the new arrival face? If all went well, he would enjoy the protection of his mother and her band for two years and maybe three, and after that he would be sent packing. Other young males, only now being born, would also find themselves in this awkward position, and he would join up with one, two, three, or even more of them to form a stud band. Together they would roam freely about the mountain, annoying harem stallions by trespassing on their home ranges and making practice raids on their harems. Not until age seven would he be capable of making a serious challenge for mares. And only if he succeeded in this endeavor would he stake out a home range and settle down.

I hoped this newborn male would live to realize every one of these normal stages of wild horse life. I hoped that his lovely mountain habitat would be preserved for him and for generations of wild horses to come. But with competition for land resources becoming ever more pressing, and human numbers growing by the second, it will take a lot of caring by a lot of people to assure that space will be provided for future wild horse herds.

While pondering these things, I caught sight of a stallion across the chasm and watched him slowly graze his way to within a few yards of the mare. He was larger than most mustangs, reddish in color, with a faded gray mane and four white stockings. Where had he come from? And what was he doing at a birth site?

Perhaps the dun mare was a member of his harem and he had come to retrieve her—odd behavior, but within the realm of possibility. But where then were his other mares? And what stallion would leave his entire band of females unguarded while he went looking for a single one that was on maternity leave?

Then something stirred in my memory. I recalled hearing ranchers tell of lone stallions staking out mares who had gone off to foal. Was that what I was seeing? What the ranchers said was this: A bachelor stud may hang around a mare and her newborn for days—just wait there for days—until the mare is ready to rejoin her old band. Then he will step right up and escort her to his own turf.

The advantage of such a tactic is obvious. Such a stallion can start a harem without having to do battle. I studied the reddish horse as he stood patiently some yards distant from the mare and her foal. He certainly was in no hurry to go anywhere. He might, in fact, have been tethered to the spot. How long would he stick around? And would this mare become so used to his presence that she would willingly go off with him?

The more I thought about it, the more convinced I became that this would happen. And it did! A few days later I spotted the threesome on a high ridge. A reddish stallion, a dun mare, and a pale buckskin foal were huddled in a tight knot and switching their tails for all they were worth. Already they had become as thick as—well, as flies. Apparently, the tales I had heard were true.

Occasionally a mare turns her maternal leave into an extended vacation. One such animal, a gorgeous creature I called Black Beauty, hung out with her dusky colt for four months at the base of the Pryor Mountains. While there she was besieged by suitors. Whether she mated with any of them, I don't know. What I do know is that none succeeded in herding her off to his harem. For some reason this female just wanted to be alone. I should have named her Greta Garbo.

Such observations have led me to two conclusions: Mares play a significant role in determining their fates; and all horses, regardless of their sex or age, can be counted on to behave in unpredictable ways.

And those are just two more of the many reasons why I find horse watching so fascinating.

This new mother is keeping a wary eye on me.

When insects become unbearable, harem mares huddle together to shield parts of their bodies.

Horse talk! Communication of some kind is taking place between a stallion and a mare. The mare is still wearing her winter coat.

A mare suckles her new foal, while her yearling filly grooms her.

Two studs nibble each other (left). *Frequent touching and mutual grooming help cement their friendship.*

A yearling expresses annoyance with a too-rambunctious foal.

Too weak to run, a newborn totters after its mother when I accidentally come upon them.

Oh joy! Happiness is a mustang foal!

In the words of cowboy-author Will James, "They really belong, not to man, but to the country of junipers and sage and deep arroyos, mesas and freedom." He regretted his early days as a wild-horse hunter.

The Return of the Native

L*ong ago, before the horse was a horse*, it was a tiny creature, no bigger than a fox, and it lived in what is now North America. That was about fifty million years ago, when the climate was very different from what it is today. Swamps and bogs dotted the land, and these were surrounded by forests of ferns as big as trees, and slipping about amid all this damp vegetation was the merest hint of a horse.

You might ask how we can know that such a creature existed. We know because its fossilized bones have been unearthed from dry canyons and sage deserts in the western United States. These ancient bones have been assembled and studied by scientists who named the little creature *Eohippus*, meaning dawn horse.

Of course, *Eohippus* did not yet look like a horse. It had four toes on its forefeet and three toes on its hind feet, and its eyes were set close together on the front of its face. Nevertheless, over eons of time, this tiny creature adapted and readapted to shifts in climate, the advance and retreat of polar ice caps, and changes in vegetation. Again and again it made itself over. Little by little it grew bigger. Little by little it lost all but one toe on each foot. And little by little it acquired teeth suitable for chewing the grasses which gradually replaced the jungle foliage that had been its diet.

All these changes can be seen in a great hall at the American Museum of Natural History in New York City. There, lined up, are the fossilized remains of every stage of this long and complex evolutionary process, from tiny *Eohippus* to mighty *Equus*, the true horse.

The oldest fossil is the fifty-five-million-year-old skeleton of *Eohippus*, the dawn horse. Its cocker spaniel–sized descendant *Mesohippus* is also on display. *Mesohippus* came into being around forty million years ago and lived until twenty million years ago. By then it had gradually transformed itself into a longer-necked, three-toed, pony-sized animal named *Merychippus*. *Merychippus*, in turn, gave rise to *Hipparion* between fifteen and sixteen million years ago. Although *Hipparion* still retained three toes, only one of them touched the ground. Finally, about two million years ago, *Equus*, the true horse, emerged. Each of *Equus*'s feet possesses only one toe, which terminates in a large hoof.

For nearly two million years *Equus*, the true horse, lived and thrived in North America. But then something strange happened. Around ten thousand years ago it became extinct on the continent, the very place that had shaped it.

Much mystery surrounds its extinction here. Most experts believe that early Indians played a part in it, for fossilized remains of charred horse bones have been found at many of their cooking sites. Some scientists, however, speculate that a plague or a global catastrophe of some kind wiped out North America's native horse. Perhaps several factors were responsible. Whatever the cause, *Equus* did indeed vanish from the landscape—and quite suddenly.

That, however, is not the end of the story. Fortunately, before *Equus* became extinct here, wave after wave of horses found their way to Asia. They traveled across a land bridge that connected Alaska and Siberia during periods when seas were shallow. Once on Asian soil, they flourished and quickly spread to the Middle East, North Africa, and Europe. Thus, fifty-five million years of evolution in North America did not end in oblivion. The horse was saved and would one day be returned to its native land.

The horse that came back to North America did not do so under its own power. During its absence the land bridge that had from time to time connected Siberia to Alaska became inundated by higher sea levels and no longer served as a thoroughfare for wandering animals and people. As a result, the very first horses to return to their native land were brought here by a Spanish explorer named Hernando Cortez just twenty-seven years after Columbus found his way to the New World. A member of this expedition, Bernal Díaz del Castillo, described these animals in his diary. He wrote:

> And the horses were divided up among the ships and loaded; mangers erected and a store of maize and hay put aboard. Captain Cortez had a dark chestnut stallion that died when we reached San Juan Ulúa. . . . Moron had a pinto with white stockings on his forefeet, well reined. . . . Diego de Ordas had a barren gray mare, a pacer who therefore seldom ran. . . . Ortez, the musician, and Bartolomé García, who had gold mines, had a

> black horse called El Arriero and he was one of the best horses taken in the fleet. . . . Sixteen horses were brought plus one foal born to the brown mare owned by Sedeña.

It goes without saying that these were not wild horses. Horses had by that time been domesticated, and special breeds had been developed to serve a variety of purposes—big ones for pulling loads, smaller ones for riding and to carry men into battle. The type of horse the Spanish explorers had aboard their ship was a Spanish-Barb, and it was tough. It had to be in order to survive a three-month sea crossing hoisted in a sling. Following this ordeal the horse had to get onto its feet and then carry one quarter of its weight while breaking trail through virgin wilderness.

The Spanish-Barb was a mix of breeds. The Barb part of its ancestry was developed in the harsh deserts of North Africa from Arabian stock. This type of horse had more than proven its mettle in the year 711 when the Moors rode it to victory over Spain. The defeated Spaniards, noting the superiority of their conqueror's horse, soon adopted it for their own use and even improved upon it. They added a touch of Norse Dun to the strain, and what emerged was the Spanish-Barb, a sure-footed creature with great stamina. This was the horse of the conquest, the animal that made it possible for Spanish conquistadors to acquire vast tracts of North and South America and subdue any Indians who stood in the way of their quest for gold.

At first the Indians of the North American Southwest and the Great Plains were amazed by the sight of an animal that would allow a man to ride on its back. As time passed, however, they came to realize that they too could sit astride a horse, and they began to appropriate any mounts the Spaniards left unguarded.

Horses dramatically changed the Indians' way of life. Hunters no longer had to stalk bison on foot—a tedious, dangerous, and time-consuming activity. On horseback the chase became easy and enjoyable and left the Plains tribes more leisure time in which to invent ceremonial dances, decorate their tepees and moccasins, and create feather headdresses. A rich culture ensued. As for the tribes in the Southwest, the possession of horses enabled them to rout the Spaniards who had colonized their sacred lands, and they drove these interlopers below the Rio Grande into what is now Mexico.

It is hard to picture the western Indians without enormous herds of horses surrounding their encampments. To them horses became symbols of wealth and power, and chiefs and braves couldn't own too many. Horses were the spoils of intertribal warfare. Horses were given as peace offerings. Horses were acquired by theft. Horses were exchanged as wedding gifts. Horses were traded northward from tribe to tribe. Warriors were so enamored of their horses that they spent long hours decorating their manes and tails with talismans and painting their bodies. In short, horses came to mean many things to the Plains Indians—who, not surprisingly, became riders without equal.

Yet despite all this the Indians were careless herdsmen. They neither castrated nor tethered their animals, and untold numbers of stallions slipped away to become wild, taking mares with them. No breed could have made this transition with as much ease as did the horse of the conquest. Its desert ancestry served it well in waterless places and where feed was short. And where grasses were lush, the horse-gone-wild thrived. By the beginning of the nineteenth century enormous herds dotted the western landscapes. It was the heyday of the wild horse. But this was not to last.

Shortly after the Civil War large numbers of dislocated Americans moved westward into what, according to treaty, was supposed to have been "Indian territory forever" and began consuming, altering, or destroying what they found there. In this venture the United States government offered its assistance: Indians were moved onto distant reservations, and their beloved ponies were either destroyed or left behind to join the wild herds.

At the same time, wild horses were also targeted. Livestock growers viewed them as competition for available grass and shot them on sight. Settlers, looking for a source of income, rounded them up and sold them for their hides or to be processed into chicken feed. Then at the turn of the century, a new market opened. Hundreds of thousands of mustangs were gathered and shipped overseas to serve as food or as mounts in the Boer War.

Not all those who pioneered the West, however, favored these actions. Some appreciated the mustang, especially when they discovered that it could be broken to work and made a first-rate cow pony. As time passed, however, these champions of the wild horse were outnumbered, and the massacre of the mustangs escalated.

There seemed no way to end it. Over many decades people chased, maimed, or killed wild horses without fear of penalty. No wildlife regulations protected the animal, for it was argued that the horse had once been domesticated and, therefore, it was not covered by laws that safeguarded other wild species. Moreover, since *Equus* wasn't present when Columbus landed, it was classified as an introduced species, alien to our native ecosystems and, therefore, a threat to our native animals.

What was the logic behind this thinking? Hadn't North America been the birthplace and cradle of *Equus* throughout every one of its evolutionary stages? And prior to its disappearance from the continent, had it not lived in harmony with native elk and bison and deer and mountain sheep? How then had it suddenly become a threat to these same animals?

But livestock growers wanted more grass for their herds, and sportsmen wanted more game to hunt. Wild horses were thought to be in the way of these goals, and they had to go. On behalf of these special interests, the United States Grazing Service (later renamed the Bureau of Land Management) set up eradication programs and paid mustangers to round up and dispose of the so-called feral horses.

From the air, it was easy to locate herds and stampede them from their last retreats. Screaming sirens attached to a plane's wings, together with blasts of buckshot, convinced even the most reluctant lead mare to abandon her home range and head into open country, where men in vehicles waited to drive the panicked animals into makeshift corrals. From there survivors were loaded into trucks, and those not too badly injured by the rough handling were driven to slaughterhouses.

By 1970 wild horses had declined to such a low number that experts predicted they would be gone within a decade. But the reaction of the public and the press to this prospect was heartening. Two weeks after my book *America's Last Wild Horses* came into print, the *New York Times* carried a front-page article about the mustangs' plight, and nearly every large newspaper in the country picked up the story. Radio and television programs invited friends of the wild horse to appear and discuss the issue. Congress was inundated by a blitz of mail, much of it from children.

With interest at such a pitch, a law to protect the mustang was all but guaranteed. And indeed, within one year the Wild Free-Roaming Horse and Burro Act was passed, which put an end to the running, killing, and selling of wild free-roaming horses living on our public lands. In the language of this law, the animal was given a unique designation. It was named our National Heritage Species.

It certainly earned that distinction. The horse was on scene during every phase of the exploration and opening of the West. Recent DNA tests performed on four wild horse herds trace the animals' lineage all the way back to the tough mounts ridden by Spanish conquistadors some four hundred years ago. As trail breakers, buffalo runners, Indian warhorses, cavalry mounts, packhorses, and cow ponies, the mustang has certainly earned its place on our public lands, as well as in our history books. It is a living monument to our rich and colorful history and deserves to be preserved.

Equally worth celebrating is the return of this native animal to the continent that gave rise to it. The sight of it running wild and free on landscapes where the very dust it kicks up may contain the pulverized remains of its earliest forms is something to marvel about. The wild horse has come full circle. *Equus* is home again.

The Colors of Horses

In the section that follows, I have used western color terminology to describe the mustangs I learned to recognize in the Pryor Mountains. Not everyone will agree with me, for how a person sees color is highly subjective: What to my eyes appears to be a dun horse may look like a buckskin to somebody else. In addition, certain color names differ from region to region. What most westerners would call a sorrel horse is generally called a chestnut in the East.

Noting color is the first step a horse-watcher must take if he hopes to recognize individual animals within a wild horse herd. Since several horses in a herd will be the same shade, however, it is necessary to observe other features as well, such as the color of the mane and tail and any white marks that appear on an animal's face and legs.

Facial marks are most helpful, since wild horses often stand behind scrub or in tall grass that obscures their legs. These are as follows:

Star Any blob of white on the horse's forehead, be it round, diamond-shaped, or just a squiggle.

Snip A tiny pink or white mark on the horse's nose.

Blaze A white band down the horse's face.
Streak A narrow trickle of white down the horse's face.
Bald face A white blaze that extends over the horse's muzzle.

The following leg marks, when visible, will clinch your identification:

Sock White hoof, coronet, and perhaps fetlock.
Half sock White extending halfway up the leg.
Stocking White extending all the way up the animal's leg.

Of course, you must make every effort to note which leg or legs wear socks, half socks, or stockings—whether front or back, left or right. Any marks on the left side of a horse are said to occur on the near side. Marks on the horse's right side are said to occur on the animal's *off* side.

Bear in mind that certain horses may appear to change color seasonally when they grow or shed their winter coats. And some horses will even change color permanently as the years pass. Black horses, for example, may fade to gray and eventually turn white with age.

Finally, do not even try to guess what color a foal will grow up to be. When it sheds its baby coat, a darker one will likely grow in. Not always, however. Black foals often become lighter as they mature.

BUCKSKIN

Body the color of tanned deer hide. Mane, tail, and lower legs black.

WHITE BUCKSKIN

Body white. Mane, tail, and lower legs black.

LIGHT GRULLA
(also called dove-colored grulla)

Body an odd shade of blue-tan. Mane and tail dark or streaked. A dark stripe runs down horse's spine and bracelets ring its legs.

DARK GRULLA
(also called mouse-colored grulla)

Similar to a light grulla, except body is gray-tan.

PINTO

A horse with spots. Example shown is a Medicine Hat pinto, named for the dark bonnet on its head and the dark shield on chest. A sacred war horse to the Cheyenne people.

DARK BAY

Dark brown body with reddish-brown highlights on underbelly, flanks, and muzzle. All bay horses, regardless of shade, must have black manes, tails, and legs. White socks are permissible.

LIGHT BAY

A light reddish-brown horse. Legs, mane, and tail are black.

MAHOGANY BAY

A bay horse with beautiful red and purple highlights.

STANDARD BROWN

Mane and tail match brown body. No reddish highlights on muzzle, flanks, or underbelly.

BLUE ROAN

A mix of black and white hairs creates the appearance of blue body. Mane and tail are black. Face and legs either black or blue.

STRAWBERRY ROAN

A mix of brown and white hairs creates the appearance of red body. Mane and tail either streaked or reddish-brown.

JET BLACK

An intense black, very shiny. Coat will not fade from sunburn or age.

BLACK-BROWN

A flat black. Some parts of this coat may fade to dark brown seasonally or with age.

DUN

Dull tan. Resembles a buckskin that has rolled in dust. Most duns have bracelets on legs and a stripe down spine. Manes and tails either black or streaked.

COPPER DUN

A red version of dun, except that the horse's mane and tail match body. Faint traces of bracelets may occur on legs.

PALOMINO

Body the color of 22-karat gold (horse on left). *Mane and tail white or nearly so.*

PALOMINO CREMELO

A cream-colored horse. Mane and tail must be white.

STANDARD SORREL

Orange body with matching orange mane and tail. In the East this color is called chestnut.

BRIGHT FLAXEN-MANED SORREL

Orange body with white mane and tail.

BLOND-SORREL

Pale orange body with light mane. This horse is often mistaken for a Palomino.

Sources

Cothran, E. Gus. "Genetic Analysis of Horses from the Pryor Mountain Wild Horse Reserve." Equine Blood Typing Research Laboratory. Department of Veterinary Science. University of Kentucky, Lexington, KY, 1992.

Cunninghame Greene, Robert Bontine. *Horses of the Conquest.* Norman: University of Oklahoma Press, 1949, pp. 118, 133.

Denhardt, Robert. "The Truth About Cortez's Horses." Translated from the Spanish text of Bernal Díaz by Genro Garcia, 1904. *Hispanic American Review* 17 (1937), pp. 525-32.

Dobie, J. Frank. *The Mustangs.* New York: Branhall House, 1934.

———, ed. *Mustangs and Cowponies.* Austin, Texas Folklore Society, 1940.

Green, Ben K. *The Color of Horses.* Northland Press, 1974.

Haines, Francis. "How Did the Indians Get Their Horses?" *American Anthropologist* 40 (1938).

Henry, Marguerite. *All About Horses.* New York: Random House, 1962, 1967.

Ryden, Hope. *America's Last Wild Horses*. New York: E. P. Dutton, 1970.

———. Revised and updated. New York: Viking Press, 1978.

———. Revised and updated. New York: Lyons and Burford, 1990.

———. *Mustangs: A Return to the Wild*. New York: Viking Pess, 1972.

———. Revised and updated. Missoula, MT: Mountain Press Publishing Company, 1984.

———. "On the Track of the West's Wild Horses." *National Geographic* (January 1971).

———. "Goodbye to the Wild Horse?" *Reader's Digest* (May 1971).

———. "The Last Wild Horses." *Children's Day* (June 1971).

Sponenberg, D. Phillip. Veterinary College, Blacksburg, VA, 24061. "North American Colonial Spanish Horse Update" (August 1992).

———. "Evaluation of Pryor Mountain Herd Area BLM Horses" (August 1993).

Wild Free-Roaming Horse and Burro Act. Public Law 92.195, 92nd Congress. S1116 (December 15, 1971).

WITHDRAWN

J
599.
66551
R

Ryden, Hope.
Wild horses I have known

18.00

WITHDRAWN

WITHDRAWN

SEP 03 1999

Manhasset Public Library
Manhasset, NY 11030
Telephone: 627-2300

WITHDRAWN

DEMCO